The lacquer of Suzuki Mutsumi and Suzuki Misako

Japanska lackarbeten av Mutsumi och Misako Suzuki

Catalogue of an exhibition
held in the
Östasiatiska Museet, Stockholm
26 March – 29 May 1988
and the
Ashmolean Museum, Oxford
21 June – 7 August 1988

O.R. Impey

Ashmolean Museum, Oxford

Text and illustrations © Ashmolean Museum, Oxford 1988
All rights reserved
ISBN 0 907849 73 3

Ashmolean Museum Publications
Oriental art

Chinese Ceramics
Eastern Ceramics from the Collection of Gerald Reitlinger
Oriental Lacquer
Japanese netsuke

Östasiatiska Museets utställningskatalog nr 47
Museum of Far Eastern Antiquities, Exhibition catalogue no. 47

Cover illustration: Eight-lobed shallow bowl, no. 13

Designed by Cole design unit, Reading
Set in Frutiger by Meridian Phototypesetting Limited
and printed in Great Britain by Henry Ling Limited,
The Dorset Press, 1988

Foreword by Jan Wirgin

Director
Museum of Far Eastern Antiquities
Stockholm

When the Museum of Far Eastern Antiquities exhibited the lacquer work of Mutsumi and Misako Suzuki in 1976, it was the first time these two young artists had had the opportunity of showing their work outside Japan. The Stockholm exhibition was highly successful and was followed by a series of outstanding exhibitions in both Europe and the Far East.

Mutsumi Suzuki, the seventh generation of a line of lacquer artists from Kyoto, has preserved not only the style and taste of his predecessors but also the traditional methods of manufacture – which although requiring much time and meticulous care are essential in maintaining the quality of the wares at the highest possible level.

Many of the pieces produced by Mutsumi and Misako Suzuki are intended for use in the tea ceremony – or *chanoyû* – and its associated *kaiseki* meal and are remarkable for their strict adherence to tradition in both form and decoration. In them, technical excellence combines with the aesthetic perfection which makes this particular type of lacquerware so outstanding.

However, while remaining faithful to tradition the artists have also broken new ground, introducing new techniques and creating new shapes and décors. Over the last few years they have been strongly influenced by the ceramics of China, particularly by the classic wares of the Sung, whose pleasingly simple forms are eminently suitable for reproduction in lacquer. On my visits to the artists' studio near the Entsuji temple on the slopes of northern Kyoto, I have always been delighted by the sense of refinement and natural simplicity with which they have instilled their new pieces. It is thus with great pleasure that I am now able to reintroduce their art to the Swedish public.

We are most fortunate to have had the assistance of the Ashmolean Museum of Oxford in organizing the exhibition, and I would like to extend special thanks to Dr. Oliver Impey who kindly agreed to draw up the catalogue and was helpful in every way in making the exhibition a reality. Warm thanks must also go to our sponsors in Japan – without their generous contributions this exhibition would never have been possible.

Foreword by O.R. Impey

Suzuki Mutsumi and Suzuki Misako, whose work is described in this catalogue, and shown in this exhibition, are a man and wife partnership. Suzuki Mutsumi is a son of the well known lacquer artist Hyosaku (1874–1942) and was, as it were, born into the craft. He is the lacquerer and the designer of the shapes; Mrs Suzuki, Suzuki Misako is the decorator of those pieces that bear any decorative effect. Their workshop is in the northern outskirts of Kyoto, for centuries the source of the finest lacquerware.

It was Dr Jan Wirgin who first suggested that this exhibition should be organised by and held in the two institutions, the Östasiatiska Museet, Stockholm, and the Ashmolean Museum, Oxford. Although the Suzukis have exhibited in Europe before, this is the first show of their own. In October 1987, I was able to visit the Suzukis in their workshop, when together we chose the items to be displayed. Much of the information in this brief account was gathered then, but any inaccuracies are my own.

Many of the pieces shown have passed out of the ownership of the Suzukis; to the lenders of these, and most particularly to the owner of the famous cake-shop Muryō-an, we are grateful. The photographs were taken by Mr Tanaka Gakuji.

For reasons of space, it may not be possible to exhibit all of the items described in this catalogue in one or other Museum.

The lacquer of
Suzuki Mutsumi and
Suzuki Misako

True lacquer is made from the sap of a tree, Rhus vernicifera, native to China and introduced into Japan. Tapped almost like maple syrup, the lacquer can be clarified or coloured to form a decorative and extremely resilient waterproof surface. As this is a surface only, it requires a supporting body; traditionally this has been wood, basketwork or textile, though leather and metal and some other substances (e.g. *papier maché*) have also been used.

Lacquer is applied to a surface with a brush, in repeated coats that may be polished before application of the next coat. The lower layers may be made thicker by the addition of ash or *tonoko* clay, when they can be modelled with a spatula. Usually a wood body, the most commonly used support, will be covered in linen or ramie cloth with the application of the first or second coat, if the piece is of any size. A variation of this technique – *kanshitsu*, dry lacquer – was used in the 8th century in Japan for large Buddhistic statues, where the armature could be removed at completion.

Natural lacquer is a rich brown colour – see no. 3 – and it can be either clarified or coloured. If it is clarified, to become transparent, it will be used as a covering surface over coloured lacquer or over some form of addition to a lacquered surface or it can itself hold in suspension coloured particles of metal, or metal dust. In early times the main colours used were cinnabar red and wood-ash carbon black, and these are still by far the most commonly used colours. Other colours, mostly first used in Edo period Japan, are based on mineral pigments. When used simply in layers of different colours, one or more layers can be cut or polished away to reveal another colour underneath; incised lacquer, in use in China at least since the 15th century was either pictorial, or pattern-making (*guri*). In Japan the polishing away of the red upper layer to reveal the black layers below, a 16th century innovation, is called *negoro*. This technique, often here used in reverse, is the basis for most of the household wares and tea ceremony utensils that are the major part of Suzuki's work and of this exhibition.

The woods used are *keaki* (Zelkova sp.), *hinoki* (Cypress), *sakura* (Prunus), and *tsugi* (Cryptomeria japonica). *Keaki* is difficult to obtain in sizes which are large enough for the larger pieces for which it is usually used, yet which are close-grained. It has, therefore, to be obtained from northern Japan, where the climate is cold enough for the trees to be slow-growing.

Hinoki is good for carving and joinery, and is light in weight, while cherry is the choice for turned pieces that have to be very thin-walled. *Tsugi* is used for flat dishes and trays.

In the Edo period, with its new and voracious demand for exquisite small works of art not made of precious materials, craftsmanship rose to new heights. The techniques of the decoration of lacquer or with lacquer were enormously varied – many of them can be seen in this exhibition applied to the tea-containers, *natsume*, mostly of the traditional shape used in *cha no yu* the tea 'ceremony', that form one part of this exhibition.

The making of *natsume* – that is the making before the decoration – exemplifies the necessary collaboration between lacquerer and the maker of the body. In the case of *natsume*, this is a wood-turner, in other cases it may be a wood-carver, or it may be both. The wood core of the *natsume* is made of *keaki* wood. When turned, the wood is so thin that it is flexible and translucent. Readers of this catalogue will notice that there are two standard types shown here, and that their measurements do not vary. The turned body and its lid, when dried weigh about 15 grams; when lacquered they will weigh about 70. Such lidded pieces must be left in a half-finished state for at least eight years, to ensure even drying.

Suzuki Mutsumi emphasises the need for close collaboration with the two woodworkers with whom he most often collaborates. Not only is the choice of the species of wood important for each different shape, so, of course, is the choice of wood of the correct grain. In particular is this true because Suzuki uses a technique of moulding the turned body by use of a simply-shaped cut-out pattern into which to press the body which will be steamed to hold it shape. Such moulded pieces become five or four sided, and could be asymmetrical. In each case, the forcing inward of one part of the body wall makes it rise slightly above the level of the 'corners'. This gives the outline a slightly wavy look, which gives motion to the whole shape. It is seen to best advantage in tall shapes such as no. 20 or the sake-Cup no. 46. In the case of lidded containers – see nos. 5 and 6 – this has to be eliminated to ensure a good fit. Because of this, there can be no turned flange, for the lid to fit over, on the body, and it has to be built up by the lacquerer, in a technique that will be described below.

The Suzukis also use a technique of joining segments of a turned body together to form a lobed shape. If it is the major part, then bilobed shapes can be made (no. 33 and 37) if smaller segments, then multiple lobed shapes are made. In one case (no. 36) the body has been cut vertically and the tops joined. When measured, these lobed pieces demonstrate how the piece of the original turned shape left unused in the making of one piece, can be used to make another; see, for instance, nos. 31 and 33.

Such is their pleasure in these re-shaped pieces, that the Suzukis are sometimes teased by their fellow artists in Kyoto, for so rarely making a round shape. Actually, of course, as this exhibition shows, there are plenty of round shapes. The making of angles does increase the difficulty of the actual lacquering process, and in particular makes the polishing of interior angles troublesome. For the exterior angles of petalled bowls, and for the lips of bowls, the polishing away of the outer layer to reveal a contrasting colour below, in the style of the old *negoro* lacquer, is almost a Suzuki mannerism. It serves to emphasise the shape.

Suzuki sometimes uses a shape, even a turned shape, where it is necessary to augment the body. In some cases, e.g. no. 38, the whole foot had to be built up without the support of a wood core; in other cases a flange within a rim, or an area around the well of a dish must be built up. Suzuki is able to do this by modelling, using a mixture of a fine clay called *tonoko*, lacquer and water. This is built up in stages and polished to the required shape.

Modelling is also required, though here in very thin layers, when a turned bowl is to be petalled, where there is a series of slightly inwardly projecting areas at the lip of a bowl – see, e.g. nos 8 and 9. In this case, the concave area is polished or cut away, while the convex area is built up. So marked may this petalling be, that a complete area of wood may actually be removed, so that the corresponding area may be built up in lacquer. As we have seen, very often Suzuki gives those areas an extra emphasis by polishing away a top coat to reveal an undercoating in a contrasting colour.

Most of the lacquers here exhibited, and, indeed most of the lacquers of Suzuki Mutsumi are decorated only by the *negoro* method, accentuating the shape. Some, however, are decorated, using a wide range of styles and techniques. This decoration is the work of Mrs Suzuki, Suzuki Misako. The success of this partnership of lacquerer and decorator can be seen most clearly in the final section of this catalogue, that devoted to the *natsume* for the tea ceremony.

Lacquer decoration requires not only the mastery of many skills, but the ability to use them in a way that gives something new to older styles. Most of the great variety of techniques developed in Japan by lacquerers of the Edo period can be seen in this exhibition. Suzuki Misako prides herself on her skill, talking dispassionately about difficulties surmounted; she is prepared to use old motifs and styles – see, for instance, no. 59, the 'kite' *natsume* and no. 54 the 'dragonflies' *natsume* – or to adapt old motifs in a subtle yet highly decorative way. The double image of the moon created by the off-centre shift of the lid of the 'autumn' *natsume* (no. 55) is perfectly suggested.

Edo lacquer techniques included much use of metallic powders, usually silver or gold of differing colours, with the particle size varying from fine powder, mostly used in *togidashi* (flat, polished-out inlay) through *nashiji* (aventurine) of varying sizes, to the cut flakes of *kirikane*. *Kirikane* is usually used to provide an extra reflecting surface to highlight some decorative element – see, for instance, the wings of the 'dragonfly' *natsume*, no. 54; *togidashi* is best seen in no. 60. Suzuki's use of *nashiji* is most interesting; she often (no. 25 and no. 55) uses it to create a double depth of pattern. This is a typical Edo period design idea, but Suzuki's use is quite original. The basis of all these techniques is *makie* – literally, sprinkled pictures or painting – a word that has now come to refer to almost all painted lacquer, but still really refers to the method of application of the metallic powder to wet, and therefore very sticky lacquer. Mrs Suzuki explains it clearly: a dry brush is used to pick up the particles; when held in position over the area to be sprinkled, the brush is tapped gently with a finger, scattering some or all of the particles off the hairs of the brush.

Lacquer painting in relief has long been a favourite device – see no. 53 – and Mrs Suzuki has employed it here in a method suggested by the *anhua* decoration ('concealed' decoration) on Chinese porcelain. In the covered boxes and bowls nos 5, 6 and 50 there is a low relief decoration entirely covered over in the final black coat of lacquer; it is only by movement either of the viewer or of the object, that the decoration becomes easily visible. In contrast to this are the high-relief inlays in iridescent pearl shell (Haliotis sp.) to be seen on nos 55 and 58, or, more muted, on no. 54. Metallic colour ground can be produced either by the suspension of metal powder in clear lacquer, or by the scattering of powder onto wet lacquer, in the same way as in *nashiji*, but to completion. Gold or silver foil was used in the Edo period, but it has a tendency to peel off, and Mrs Suzuki does not favour its use.

Suzuki Mutsumi's work exemplifies the collaboration between lacquerer and body-maker. The collaboration with his wife for the decoration of his works adds another dimension to this successful co-operation.

1

1   Large turned covered dish
     1985
Horizontal bands made by the turner have been
used to give this large serving bowl an even greater
impression of width. The red exterior conceals a
black interior.
     h. 17 cm
     w. 47 cm

•   9

2

3

2   Large turned and carved covered dish
    1983
The almost brutal strength of this bowl is
emphasised by the petal carving of the sides of both
the bowl and the lid, done by a wood-carver after
the bodies were turned, and by the strong foot ring.
The coarse matt black surface is made by a build-up
of ash and lacquer, covered in a rice-husk paper
soaked in lacquer. This large serving bowl has ten
small bowls en suite (some of which are shown here,
see no. 26).
The owner, a celebrated Kyoto cake-maker, uses this
at New Year festivities.
Exhibited Taipei 1983
    h. 23.4 cm
    w. 51.3 cm

3   Square cake-box with canted corners
    1976
This box is a variation of a classic shape, covered in
natural lacquer to give this rich brown effect.
    h. 9.3 cm
    w. 19.5 cm

4

5

6

4   Lobed covered cake-box
     1986
The shape of this black covered box, with its
suggestion of plum-blossom, is made by the joining
together of segments cut from a turned shape. This is
an innovation of Suzuki Mutsumi, and can be seen
also in no. 9.
The layer of black lacquer that covers this box is
polished at the edges to reveal the red lacquer
underneath.
     h. 11.2 cm
     w. 14.8 cm

5   Rounded covered cake-box
     1986
There is a 'concealed' decoration of three flowers
under the matt black surface, made by Suzuki
Misako. This box could be used for *manju* bean cakes
for 5 persons.
     h. 12.3 cm
     w. 14.4 cm

6   Square covered cake-box with rounded corners
     1983
A built-up shape, with concealed decoration by
Suzuki Misako, of *kiri-mon* (Paulownia-flower
emblems).
     h. 8.8 cm
     w. 14.2 cm

7

7   Three tiered box
    1978
Tiered boxes, *jubako*, are used at the New Year. The
shape of this box is carefully made to be just off the
square; the sides are slightly curved. The decoration
in gold lacquer by Suzuki Misako is of rice ears, on a
polished black (*roiro*) ground.
Exhibited Taipei 1983
    h. 26.4 cm
    w. 22.6 cm

8

9

---

8 Six-petalled deep bowl
   1986

The petalled shape in the red lacquer has been
achieved by the cutting-away and building-up of the
side of the bowl. So deep may this cutting go, that
the wood core may be entirely removed from the
outer edge, and the inner edge will be entirely
built-up of lacquer mixed with *tonoko* clay. A dish of
this shape could be used with hot food.

    h. 12.4 cm
    w. 37.8 cm

9 Eight-lobed bowl
   1986

Joined with smaller segments of a turned shape
than was no. 4, this bowl uses the same technique.
Emphasis is given to this, by the polishing-away of
the final black lacquer coat at the edges to reveal the
red lacquer beneath.

    h. 12.0 cm
    w. 26.0 cm

10

10   Large petal-spiralled dish
     1986
Carving of the rim into the body gives the
overlapping effect on this large red dish.
     h. 7.0 cm
     w. 40.7 cm

11

12

---

11 Shallow lobed dish
    1986
Of joined construction, this red dish could be used
for a formal *kaiseki* meal in the tea ceremony. It
conforms to the *hassun* size (a module of 8 × approx
3 cm.) that would be used to serve two small portions
of carefully arranged contrasting foods; one would
be a product of the sea, the other from wild plants
gathered in the mountains.
    h. 5.1 cm
    w. 26.0 cm

12 Five-petalled shallow dish
    1982
The petalling is cut well into the wood body, as it is
in no. 8, and has been emphasised by the polishing
of the black lacquer exterior to show a red lacquer
underneath. This could be used for serving small
cakes.
    h. 5.2 cm
    w. 21.2 cm

13

14

13 Eight-lobed shallow bowl
    1978
The joined construction is again pointed by the
polishing-away of the red final coat of lacquer to
reveal the black lacquer beneath, at all the edges.
Exhibited Brussels, Cologne, Stuttgart, London 1981
    h. 4.8 cm
    w. 16.6 cm

14 Bowl with carved petalled rim
    1976
Carving of the turned body, by a woodcarver, gives
this strongly accented petalling. The rim area is in
natural lacquer-colour, a rich brown, the lower part
is black.
    h. 7.4 cm
    w. 21.9 cm

17

15 Unfinished shallow bowl
    1987
The curve of the sides of this bowl so pleased the
Suzukis, that they were anxious to exhibit it in this
unfinished state. The final coat will be in natural
(brown) lacquer and there will be a decoration of
carefully painted silver-lacquer drips running down
the inside of the bowl, symmetrically placed.
    h. 6.5 cm
    w. 24.6 cm

16 Ten-lobed shallow bowl
    1979
The joined shape has been covered with lacquer-
soaked rice-husk paper (see also no. 2) to give the
grained black effect.
    h. 7.5 cm
    w. 26.7 cm

17 Pierced bowl in silver and gold lacquer
    1979
Both metallic effects are achieved by the suspension
of metal dust in clear lacquer. The silver ground of
the bowl is pierced by round holes, like drops of dew,
under a gold rim. This bowl would be suitable for
summer use, to serve fruit.
    h. 8.8 cm
    w. 23.1 cm

1

30d

55

32

18

18   Squared bowl, spring and autumn
     1985
The shape of this bowl has been made by the
moulding of a turned wood body. The decoration
of spring and autumn flowers in silver powder in
lacquer, by Suzuki Misako, is on a mi-parti ground of
natural lacquer and of gold lacquer under natural
lacquer.
    h. 11.5 cm
    w. 21.3 cm

19

20

---

19 Three-petalled bowl
    1986
This red bowl has been carved at the rim (as no. 4) to
suggest a Trillium flower, which has a symbolism of
long life wishes. The black lacquer underlayer shows
at the polished red edges. This is not a cup, but would
be used for green vegetables.
    h. 10.0 cm
    w. 16.3 cm

20 Moulded tall bowl
    1986
The round shape of this tall bowl has been moulded
with the use of steam to give a slightly triangular
effect, and the black surface has been polished at the
lip to reveal red underneath.
    h. 12.5 cm
    w. 14.0 cm

25

10

50

9

22

21 Five-sided rounded bowl
   1987
Pressed into a mould and steamed, the thin wood
core of this turned bowl has conformed to a
five-sided shape. The black lacquer of the surface
has been polished at the lip to reveal the red
underneath.
   h. unknown
   w. unknown

22 Five-petalled shallow dish
   1986
Carved into the wood-core (as no. 8) this shallow dish
of *hassun* size (see no. 11) is black over red.
   h. 3.3 cm
   w. 24.9 cm

23

23 Petalled dish with tall foot
    1985
The carved petalling of this black dish gives an
overlapping effect. The tall foot is a classic shape, but
has no particular purpose or significance other than
to look well.
    h. 5.5 cm
    w. 18.9 cm

19

31

40

18

25

24 Red bowl
    1986
The elegant simplicity of this bowl would make it
suitable for humble foods such as *ochazuke*.
    h. 6.4 cm
    w. 17.5 cm

25 Set of three cherry-blossom decorated dishes
    1979
The bold decoration of these dishes is in silver
lacquer, with a scattering of gold-dust (*nashiji*) for
the petal shapes, bordered by gold lacquer on a
black background. The reverse is in red.
Exhibited Taipei 1983
    h. 3.5 cm
    w. 20.3 cm

27

26 Two ten-lobed bowls with gold rims
    1983
These carved bowls are two of the single-serving
bowls en suite with the large covered bowl, no. 2.
Exhibited Taipei 1983.
    h. 5.5 cm
    w. 17.1 cm

27 Bean-shaped tray
    1987
The wooden core has been carved to give the form of
this black tray, with the undercoat of red revealed at
the lip.
    h. 1.6 cm
    w. 22.6 cm

34

6

17

47

b

28 Irregular tray
      1987
An abstract design in black over red.
      h. 2.5 cm
      w. 23.3 cm

29 Large bean-shaped tray
      1987
These trays are carved from a plank of wood, to
an outline drawn by Suzuki. Here the large size is
emphasised by the brilliant red lacquer.
      h. 2.5 cm
      w. 35.4 cm

30 Five mukozuke dishes
      1978–87
Sets of five matching *mukozuke* (small food bowls)
are a standard item of Japanese tableware. In recent
years, following, perhaps, a wave of antiquarianism,
irregular sets have become fashionable. This set of
different pieces, moulded, carved or joined was
'created' in discussion with the artist in October 1987.
a   Irregular moulded bowl, red under black, 1987
      h. 6.2 cm
      w. 13.5 cm
b   Joined five-lobed bowl, red, 1978
      h. 5.6 cm
      w. 14.2 cm

c

e

d

c   Moulded three-sided bowl, red, 1985
    h. 7.1 cm
    w. 12.1 cm
d   Three-sided moulded red bowl, 1986
The shape suggests the formalised branches of pine
trees that grow on the sea shore.
    h. 4.6 cm
    w. 15.1 cm

e   Carved petalled bowl, red, 1978
Exhibited Brussels, Cologne, Stuttgart, London 1981
    h. 6.5 cm
    w. 14.4 cm

31

32

---

31 Five-lobed dish
    1978
This red dish, and the two following items, share in
common a basic shape, in that they are joined from
segments cut from the same turned wood core
shape. This core shape lacks a foot, and it has in each
case been built up by the lacquerer.
Exhibited Brussels, Cologne, Stuttgart, London 1981
    h. 2.6 cm
    w. 17.2 cm

32 Three-lobed dish
    1978
See preceding item. The sides of this dish have been
painted with gold lacquer waves under natural
lacquer by Suzuki Misako.
    h. 2.5 cm
    w. 15.6 cm

33

34

---

33 Bi-lobed dish
   1978
See the preceding two items. The interior of the
everted rim has been decorated with rice ears in gold
lacquer, evocative of autumn, by Suzuki Misako.
   h. 2.4 cm
   w. 15.1 cm

34 Set of five five-sided moulded mukozuke dishes
   1985
The cherry-wood core has been moulded and
steamed to conform to this black lacquer
plum-blossom shape.
Shown with an untreated cherry-wood core.
   h. 4.1 cm
   w. 14.0 cm

35

36

35 Set of five squared moulded mukozuke dishes
   1985
See preceding item. These red dishes are moulded,
using exactly the same body as those of no. 34, into a
four-sided shape.
   h. 4.1 cm
   w. 13.6 cm

36 Rice-bale-shaped dish
   1979
This dish is made of two *keaki*-wood bowl shapes
fixed end to end (contrast with the following item).
The underside is ridged in natural lacquer to imitate
a rice bale, and the interior is in black polished
lacquer decorated with rice-ears.
Exhibited Taipei 1983
   h. 3.8 cm
   w. 12.5 cm

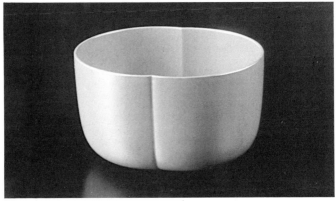

37

37   Bi-lobed bowl
1978
See preceding item. Here the same bowl shaped
keaki wood core has been cut and fixed side by side,
and decorated in red lacquer.
   h. 6.0 cm
   w. 10.7 cm

38

38   Ten-lobed dish
     1978
Of joined construction, this dish has an inner band
and a low foot built up of lacquer (mixed with
tonoko clay) without a supporting wood body. This
could be used for *hassun* dishes (see no. 11).
Exhibited Brussels, Cologne, Stuttgart, London 1981
     h. 2.7 cm
     w. 25.8 cm

39

40

39 Thirty-petalled carved dish
    1976
Although the shape is turned and then carved, the
foot is built up of lacquer in the manner of that of
the preceding item.
Exhibited Taipei 1983
    h. 2.2 cm
    w. 21.1 cm

40 Thirty-six-petalled carved dish
    1978
The many-petalled shapes used in Suzuki Mutsumi's
lacquer find their ancestry in Chinese porcelain
forms, as well as in real flower shapes. Here, black
carved petalling surrounds a red centre.
Exhibited Brussels, Cologne, Stuttgart, London 1981
    h. 3.2 cm
    w. 24.8 cm

41

43

42

---

41   Five-petalled carved small dish
      1986
Carved as in no. 8, the red under-layer shows where
the black has been polished away at the edges.
      h. 2.5 cm
      w. 13.9 cm

42   Five-petalled carved small dish
      1985
The profile of this dish is sharper than that of the
preceding item; otherwise the red over black
decoration is the reverse.
      h. 2.5 cm
      w. 12.6 cm

43   Six-petalled carved small bowl
      1983
With smoothly curving sides, this bowl has black over
red decoration.
      h. 3.6 cm
      w. 15.0 cm

44 45 46

44 Tray with handle
    1983
The form of this tray is a modification of an early
shape. The sides, waved at the top, are slightly bent
outwards; the handle is made of two thin (1 mm)
layers of *hinoki* (cypress) wood with an equally thin
layer of aluminium sandwiched in between. The
decoration, in gold lacquer, of cherry blossom and
maple leaves under natural lacquer is overlaid
asymmetrically across the centre of the base with
a broad raised thick band of black lacquer. The
underside, where the lacquer is thinner, shows the
texture of the linen cloth which covers the whole
body, but is elsewhere concealed by polishing.
    h. 26.8 cm
    w. 35.7 cm

45 Sake cup
    1982
Round red lacquer over black, with scattered
cherry-blossom in gold lacquer.
    h. 3.2 cm
    w. 4.8 cm

46 Sake cup
    1985
Red lacquer moulded into a three-sided form.
    h. 5.9 cm
    w. 4.9 cm

47

47 Six-petalled carved dish
    1983
With out-turned, deeply indented profile, this dish
is decorated in gold lacquer on the inside and with
black on the outside, utilising the technique of
lacquer-soaked paper that is used in no. 2. The gold
lacquer is a carefully applied layer of fine gold dust
under clear lacquer.
    h. 3.8 cm
    w. 15.2 cm

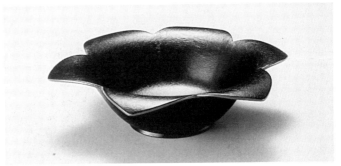

48

48 Six-petalled carved bowl
1975
Again using the paper and lacquer technique this
black bowl has a deeply everted and indented
outline, emphasised by a band of red lacquer at
the rim.
Exhibited Taipei 1983
h. 4.7 cm
w. 15.3 cm

49 *Koban*-shaped tray
1975
The shape is based on that of the old gold coins of
Japan. Originally simply cut from a flat piece of
wood, the edge of this tray has been built up by the
lacquerer from lacquer and clay, and smoothed into
the flat surface of highly polished black lacquer
(*roiro*). The underside is linen-textured.
h. 1.1 cm
w. 37.6 cm

50

50   Covered soup bowl
     1975
The standard shape for a soup bowl has the lid
that fits thus, inside the bowl. The decoration,
'concealed' under the polished black exterior is of
yusuri leaves, bringing wishes for good fortune.
Exhibited Brussels, Cologne, Stuttgart, London 1981
     h. 10.0 cm
     w. 13.7 cm

51   Covered soup bowl
     1985
In a strong shape recalling that of the large covered
bowl, no. 2, this bowl has the red underlayer of
lacquer revealed by the polishing of the black upper
layer.
     h. 7.9 cm
     w. 13.6 cm

52

Natsume

Most of the *natsume*, containers for powdered tea to be used in the tea ceremony, in this exhibition are of traditional form, and are decorated in various techniques by Suzuki Misako. The black *natsume* is of innovatory shape, in a style particularly liked by the Suzukis.

52 *Natsume* of squared form
1986

The moulded turned body of this new shape has been given a thick coating of black lacquer over red lacquer, and has a 'concealed' decoration of cranes, symbols of long life. The inner flange of the base part has been built up in lacquer. This shape, with its wide opening, tall lid and squared form has not been used as a natsume before, and is likely to appeal to the more experimental approach to the use of vessels of the tea ceremony that is now a fashion.

h. 7.5 cm
w. 8.0 cm

53

54

55

53 *Natsume*
198
The decoration of waves, with a fisherman in his
boat on the lid, has been painted in different colours
of gold lacquer on a powdered gold and silver (in the
proportion of 9–1) ground. This colour is even on
the upper surface of the lid, but there is a gradation
down the sides, like a shadow, so that the lower part
is black.
  h. 7.4 cm
  w. 7.3 cm

54 *Natsume*
1978
The black ground has been decorated in raised
lacquer in gold and colours, and with *kirigane*
(pieces of gold leaf) and pearl shell inlay, with a
pattern of dragonflies on rushes.
Exhibited Brussels, Cologne, Stuttgart, London 1981
Exhibited Taipei 1983
  h. 7.4 cm
  w. 7.3 cm

56

57

55 *Natsume*
1982
The symbols of autumn, *susuki* grass, a rabbit and the moon in gold and silver lacquers, with a rabbit in awabi shell (Haliotis) in high relief. The silver moon has a scattering of gold *nashiji*, and leaves a crescent of gold on the lid, while the gold lacquer grasses form a criss-cross pattern on the body. The pearl-shell rabbit, of traditional form, is silhouetted against the moon.
 h. 6.0 cm
 w. 8.2 cm

56 *Natsume*
1985
A Chinese boy shelters under a large lotus leaf as if it were an umbrella. The leaf covers the lid almost symmetrically, in gold lacquer while at its centre sits a 'blue-gold' frog with gold eyes. The boy's kimono has gold nashiji over red, making a contrast with the black ground.
 h. 6.0 cm
 w. 8.2 cm

57 *Natsume*
1983
The striped effect of the black ground of this natsume is made by painting on a mixture of bone-glue and lacquer with a stiff brush. The serrated effect makes it difficult to paint over, and the sparrows and bamboo have had to have many coats of lacquer, polished and re-polished. The interior is gold lacquer.
 h. 6.0 cm
 w. 8.2 cm

58

59

58 *Natsume*
    1986
'Morning flowers' in pearl shell have leaves in
blue-gold, covered in a layer of black lacquer which
is polished away almost entirely to give a very special
effect. The body is scattered with gold and silver
nashiji in a wide effect which is difficult to obtain,
especially where it has to cover two parts of an
object, as here; to get the sprinkle even is the
problem.
    h. 6.0 cm
    w. 8.2 cm

59 *Natsume*
    1979
The decoration is of a kite, such as would be used
for the Boy's Festival (5 May) or for New Year, in
traditional form, as a *yakko*, a low-ranking samurai,
who wears only one sword. The red colour is
obtained here by using a very thin coating of red
lacquer over gold lacquer. The interior is of gold
lacquer.
    h. 6.0 cm
    w. 8.2 cm

60 *Natsume*
    1982
Green clouds, made of a mixture of blue gold and
silver dust are revealed through a layer of red
lacquer by flat polishing, in the classic technique
togidashi.
    h. 7.4 cm
    w. 7.3 cm